All New Crafts for Easter

KATHY ROSS
Illustrated by Sharon Lane Holm

The Millbrook Press • Brookfield, Connecticut

For my two little chickies,
Julianna and Ashlyn.
K.R.

For James Aidan Thomas,
welcome to the world little one.
S.L.H.

Library of Congress Cataloging-in-Publication Data

Ross, Kathy (Katharine Reynolds), 1948-
All new crafts for Easter / by Kathy Ross ; illustrated by Sharon Lane Holm.
p. cm. — (All-new holiday crafts for kids)
Summary: Presents twenty simple craft projects for springtime and Easter that can be made from everyday materials.
ISBN 0-7613-2921-8 (lib. bdg.) — ISBN 0-7613-2392-9 (pbk.) 1. Easter decorations—Juvenile literature. 2. Handicraft—Juvenile literature. [1. Easter decorations. 2. Handicraft.] I. Holm, Sharon Lane, ill. II. Title. III. Series.
TT900.E2R65 2004   745.594'1667—dc22   2003011891

Published by The Millbrook Press, Inc.
2 Old New Milford Road
Brookfield, Connecticut 06804
www.millbrookpress.com

Printed in the United States of America
5 4 3 2 1 (lib. ed.)
5 4 3 2 1 (paper)

Contents

Tissue Box Basket • 4

Filter Basket • 6

Powder-Room Chick • 8

Lemon Table Chick • 10

Spring Birds Lapel Pin • 12

Bunny Family • 14

Easter Basket Bonnet • 17

String Bunny Magnet • 18

Embroidery Floss Rabbit Pin • 20

Twitching Nose Bunny Puppet • 22

Twist-Tie Flower Corsage • 24

"Eggs"-cellent Egg Pokes • 26

Basket of Flowers Door Wreath • 28

Spring Lamb Finger Puppet • 30

Eggshell Flowers • 32

Hatching Chick Wobblers • 34

Bird's Nest Favor • 36

Ribbon Flowers Garland • 38

Hatching Duck Puppet • 40

Egg Angel Wall Hanging • 42

Easter Bonnet Snack Dish • 44

Bunny and Basket Place Card • 46

A tisket, a tasket, make an Easter basket!

Tissue Box Basket

Here is what you need:

 square tissue box

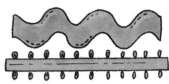 hole punch

 thin craft ribbon and trims

 white craft glue

facial tissue

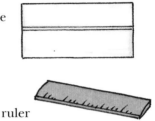

scissors

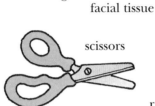

ruler

Easter grass

Here is what you do:

1 Cut around the top square of the box to remove it.

2 Cut halfway down from each of the top corners of the box. Cut across the box on opposite sides to remove the top portion of the box.

3 Make two cuts halfway down, 1 inch (2.5 cm) apart, on each of the remaining sides of the box. Cut out the piece on each side of the 1-inch strips, so that the two strips can be joined together to form the handle of the basket.

4 Punch a hole in the end of each strip. Use the scissors to round off the corners. Thread a piece of craft ribbon through the two holes and tie the ends together in a bow to form the handle.

5 Cut the facial tissue into 1-inch (2.5-cm)-wide strips. Squeeze glue around the top edge of the basket.

6 Press one side of the strips of facial tissue into the glue and pinch the top edge of the strip together as you go along, to form a tissue ruffle around the basket. Continue adding strips of gathered tissue until the entire top edge of the basket has a ruffle around it.

7 Squeeze a strip of glue over the top edge of the ruffle. Cover the glued edge with a strip of craft ribbon or trim. If there is some writing on the tissue box that you wish to cover, add another row or two of trim around the box basket.

8 Fill the basket with Easter grass. Add some Easter candy, decorated eggs, or the chick that you can make following the instructions on page 10.

The many pretty designs found on square tissue boxes make them an ideal choice for making spring baskets.

Here is another idea for a fun and easy Easter basket.

Filter Basket

Here is what you need:

scissors

glue

white craft glue

washable markers

thin craft ribbon in two colors

NEWS

newspaper to work on

paintbrush

4- to 5-inch (10- to 13-cm) disposable plastic container for drying

12-inch (30-cm) pipe cleaner in two colors

four white coffee filters

paper cup for mixing

water

Here is what you do:

1 Use the markers to make splotches of color around the edge of one of the filters.

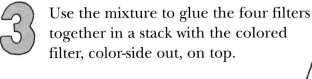

2 Mix half glue and half water in the paper cup.

3 Use the mixture to glue the four filters together in a stack with the colored filter, color-side out, on top.

4 Paint over the outside of the colored filter with the glue and water to blend the colors.

 5 Shape the filters over the bottom of the plastic container.

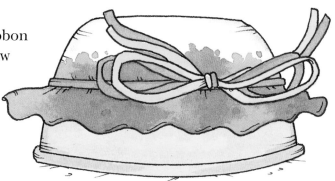

6 Tie two colors of craft ribbon around the filters in a bow about 1 inch (2.5 cm) from the edge. Fold the edge of the filter out around the ribbon to give the basket a ruffled edge.

7 Let the filters dry completely to hold the shape of the basket. Then remove it from the container.

8 Twist the two pipe cleaners together to make a handle for the basket. Glue an end of the handle all the way down each inside surface of the basket.

Fill the basket with some Easter grass and your favorite Easter treats.

7

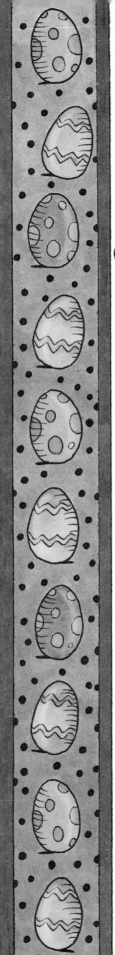

Make this quick chick project to decorate the bathroom.
Powder-Room Chick

Here is what you need:

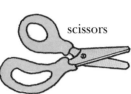

scissors

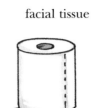
white craft glue

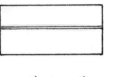
facial tissue

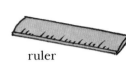
ruler

roll of toilet tissue

two 12-inch (30-cm) orange pipe cleaners

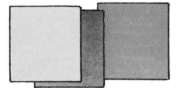
orange, black, and yellow construction paper scraps

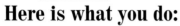

yellow and white craft feathers

Here is what you do:

1 Fold the orange paper in half and cut a triangle-shaped beak on the fold to make the top and bottom of the chick's beak.

2 Cut two 1-inch (2.5-cm) eyes for the chick from the black paper.

3 Glue the two eyes to the top part of the side of the toilet tissue roll. Glue the bottom part of the beak to the toilet tissue roll below the eyes so that the top part of the beak sticks out.

4 Cut two wings for the chick from the yellow paper. Glue a wing on each side of the toilet tissue roll with the face in the center.

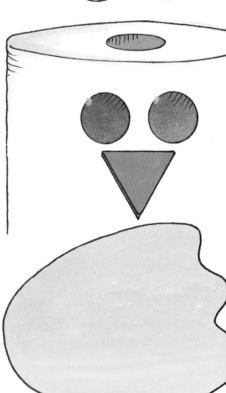
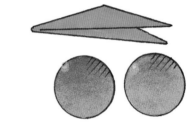

8

5 The pipe cleaners will be the two legs for the chick. Cut a 2-inch (5-cm) piece from the end of each pipe cleaner.

6 Wrap each piece around a pipe cleaner about an inch from the end to make a foot at the end of each leg.

7 Slip the end of each leg in between the layers of toilet tissue at the bottom of the chick. Arrange the legs so that they bend forward, then hang down at the front of the chick to look like the chick is sitting on the shelf.

8 Stuff a wad of facial tissue down inside the top of the toilet roll tube. Put some craft feathers in the top part of the cardboard tube, with the ends between the tissue and the cardboard to hold them in place, so they stick out of the top of the chick's head.

Cheep!

When Easter is over, just remove the outer paper on the roll and pull out the legs and feathers to use the toilet tissue roll. You might want to save the pieces to quickly construct a new chick next year.

9

Make this cheerful chick to decorate a table or display in a basket.

Lemon Table Chick

Here is what you need:

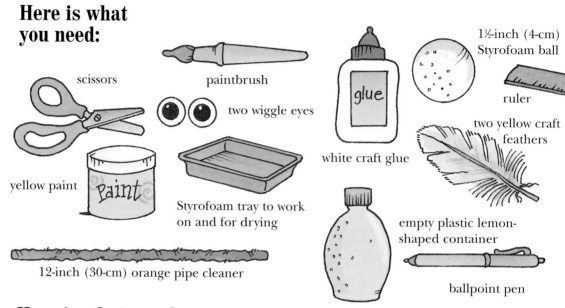

scissors

paintbrush

two wiggle eyes

yellow paint

Styrofoam tray to work on and for drying

white craft glue

glue

1½-inch (4-cm) Styrofoam ball

ruler

two yellow craft feathers

empty plastic lemon-shaped container

ballpoint pen

12-inch (30-cm) orange pipe cleaner

Here is what you do:

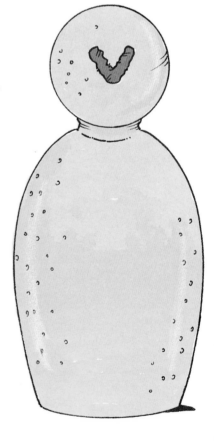

1 The plastic lemon container will become the body for the chick, and the Styrofoam ball will become the head. Twist the Styrofoam ball on over the lid of the lemon container. You might want to use the end of the pen to poke a hole in the ball to get it started. Remove the ball, add a dab of glue, and place the ball back over the lid.

2 Paint the Styrofoam ball yellow and let it dry.

3 Cut a 1-inch (2.5-cm)-long piece from the orange pipe cleaner. Fold the piece in half to form a triangle-shaped beak. Dip the two ends of the beak in glue, then press them into the front of the Styrofoam ball head of the chick.

 Glue the two wiggle eyes to the head above the beak.

5 Cut the orange pipe cleaner in half for the two legs. Cut a 2-inch (5-cm) piece from the end of each one. Wrap a piece around each pipe cleaner, about 1 inch (2.5 cm) from the end to make the feet for the chick.

6 Use the pen to poke two holes, about 1 inch (2.5 cm) apart, in the middle of one side of the chick's body.

7 Dip the end of each pipe cleaner leg in glue, then slip one into each hole. Glue a craft feather on each side of the body for the wings.

Peep! Peep!

11

Make a little flock of spring birds to wear on your coat or collar.

Spring Birds Lapel Pin

Here is what you need:

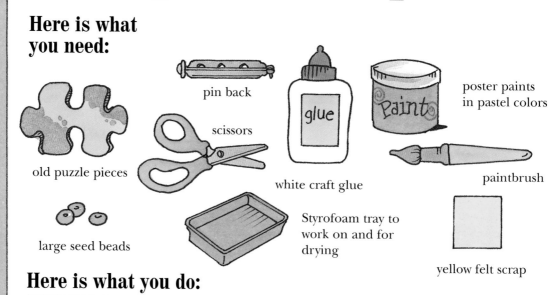

old puzzle pieces

pin back

scissors

white craft glue

glue

Paint

poster paints in pastel colors

paintbrush

large seed beads

Styrofoam tray to work on and for drying

yellow felt scrap

Here is what you do:

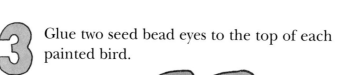

1. Choose three puzzle pieces that have two sides sticking out at the top and the bottom and a knob on each side to look like bird wings.

2. Paint the back of each puzzle piece a different color. Let the three pieces dry.

3. Glue two seed bead eyes to the top of each painted bird.

Cut a tiny triangle-shaped beak for each bird from the yellow felt.

5 Glue a beak on each bird below the eyes.

6 Arrange the birds in a flock so that they are slightly overlapping one another. When you find an arrangement you are pleased with, glue the three birds together at the contact points.

7 Glue a pin back to the back of the flock.

Peep!

You might want to try making a pin with more than three birds in the flock.

Make yourself a family of tiny bunnies to play with.

Bunny Family

Here is what you need:

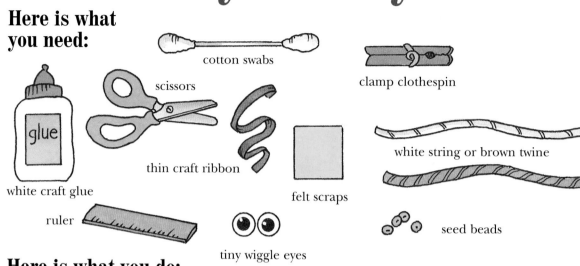

cotton swabs

scissors

clamp clothespin

glue

thin craft ribbon

white string or brown twine

white craft glue

felt scraps

ruler

tiny wiggle eyes

seed beads

Here is what you do:

1 Hold two cotton swabs together so that they are crossed just below the cotton tips.

2 Wrap white cotton string (or brown twine, depending on what color bunny you are making) around the two swabs below the cotton ends to form a head, with the two cotton ends forming ears. The bottoms of the swabs will form the legs.

3 Hold a third cotton swab across the first two to form the arms. Continue wrapping the string around the body and center of the arms to secure them to the body. Wrap to the cotton end of each arm and back to the body, to cover the stick portion of the arms.

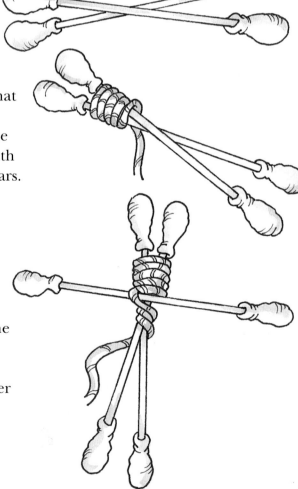

14

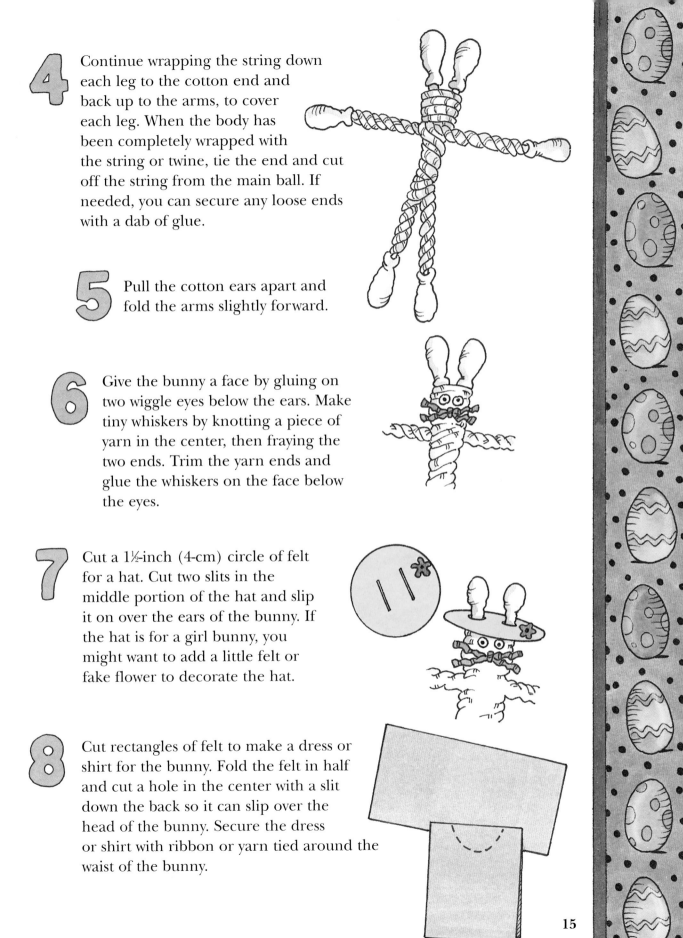

4 Continue wrapping the string down each leg to the cotton end and back up to the arms, to cover each leg. When the body has been completely wrapped with the string or twine, tie the end and cut off the string from the main ball. If needed, you can secure any loose ends with a dab of glue.

5 Pull the cotton ears apart and fold the arms slightly forward.

6 Give the bunny a face by gluing on two wiggle eyes below the ears. Make tiny whiskers by knotting a piece of yarn in the center, then fraying the two ends. Trim the yarn ends and glue the whiskers on the face below the eyes.

7 Cut a 1½-inch (4-cm) circle of felt for a hat. Cut two slits in the middle portion of the hat and slip it on over the ears of the bunny. If the hat is for a girl bunny, you might want to add a little felt or fake flower to decorate the hat.

8 Cut rectangles of felt to make a dress or shirt for the bunny. Fold the felt in half and cut a hole in the center with a slit down the back so it can slip over the head of the bunny. Secure the dress or shirt with ribbon or yarn tied around the waist of the bunny.

15

9 To make pants for a boy bunny, cut a rectangle of felt to glue around each leg.

10 Make a baby bunny by crossing two 1½-inch (4-cm) pieces cut from the ends of a cotton swab and wrapping them in string, starting below the cotton ends.

11 Glue on two seed bead eyes and wrap the baby bunny in a felt blanket. Use glue to hold the blanket in place. If it wants to pop open, secure it with a clamp clothespin until the glue is dry.

These bunnies also look very nice hanging on an egg tree. Just add a loop hanger to the back of each bunny you make.

Turn last year's Easter basket into a fancy Easter hat.

Easter Basket Bonnet

Here is what you need:

scissors

small net bag such as onions come in

pipe cleaner

one or two fake flowers

old inexpensive Easter basket that fits on your head

ruler

Here is what you do:

1 Cut the handle off the basket and flip it over to use as a hat.

2 Cut two 2-inch (5-cm) pieces of pipe cleaner. Fold the two pieces in half. These will be used to attach the net bag to the hat to look like hat netting.

3 Thread both ends of a piece of pipe cleaner through one end of the net bag and then through the edge of the basket to attach the net to the hat.

4 Attach the other side of the net in the same way.

5 Poke one or two fake flowers through the weave of the basket on one end of the net (or make ribbon flowers following the instructions found in Basket of Flowers Door Wreath on page 28).

Collect several old baskets and create an entire wardrobe of different hats to play with. You probably will have some decorating ideas of your own.

17

This little bunny is to stick on the refrigerator.

String Bunny Magnet

Here is what you need:

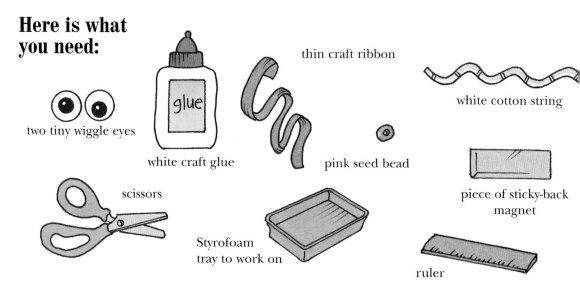

two tiny wiggle eyes

white craft glue

thin craft ribbon

pink seed bead

white cotton string

piece of sticky-back magnet

scissors

Styrofoam tray to work on

ruler

Here is what you do:

1 Cover a 3-inch (8-cm)-square area on the center of the Styrofoam tray with a layer of glue.

2 Make a circle body for the bunny by wrapping a length of string around and around itself in a spiral on the glue on the Styrofoam tray. When the body is the size you want (about 1½ inches (4-cm) wide is a good size for a magnet), trim off the excess string. If you notice a small opening in the center of the circle just snip off a tiny piece of string and press it into the glue in the opening to fill it.

3 Make a smaller circle of string in the glue on one side of the body for the head.

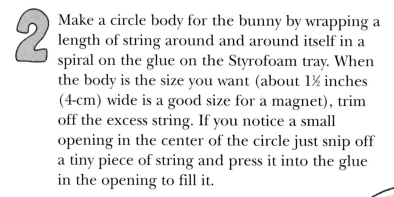

4 Make a very small circle on the opposite side for the tail.

5 Make two elongated ovals with the string on the top of the head for long bunny ears.

6 Let the glued string dry completely, then peel the bunny off the Styrofoam tray. Use the scissors to trim away any excess glue from around the edges of the bunny.

7 Glue the two wiggle eyes on the head. Glue the pink seed bead below the eyes for a nose.

8 Tie a bow with a piece of the craft ribbon and glue it to the neck of the bunny.

9 Press a piece of sticky-back magnet on the back of the bunny.

You can arrange the string circles in a different way to make a bunny in a different position.

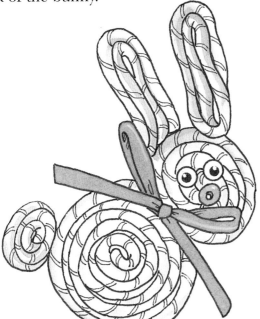

19

This Easter rabbit wants to ride on your collar.

Embroidery Floss Rabbit Pin

Here is what you need:

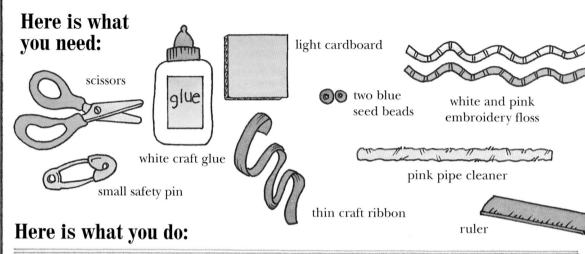

scissors

glue

white craft glue

small safety pin

light cardboard

two blue seed beads

white and pink embroidery floss

pink pipe cleaner

thin craft ribbon

ruler

Here is what you do:

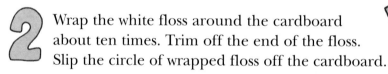

1 Cut a 2½-inch (6-cm)-square piece of cardboard.

2 Wrap the white floss around the cardboard about ten times. Trim off the end of the floss. Slip the circle of wrapped floss off the cardboard.

3 Thread a piece of white floss between the front and back parts of the circle and tie the piece in a knot to secure the wrapped floss at the top. Trim off the ends of the tied floss.

4 Cut a 4-inch (10-cm) piece of pipe cleaner for the ears. Wrap the two ends of the pipe cleaner together to make a circle, then shape the two sides into two ears.

5 Slide the ears in between the front and the back of the tied floss so that they stick up on each side of the top.

6 Tie a piece of ribbon around the floss, about ½ inch (1.27 cm) down from the ears, to make a neck for the rabbit. Tie the ribbon in a bow.

7 Wrap some white floss around the card about five times to make the arms for the rabbit. Slip the wrapped floss off the card.

8 Tie the arms on each side where you want the wrist to be. Make the arms shorter than the body is tall to make them look in proportion. Trim off the folded floss at each end of the arms.

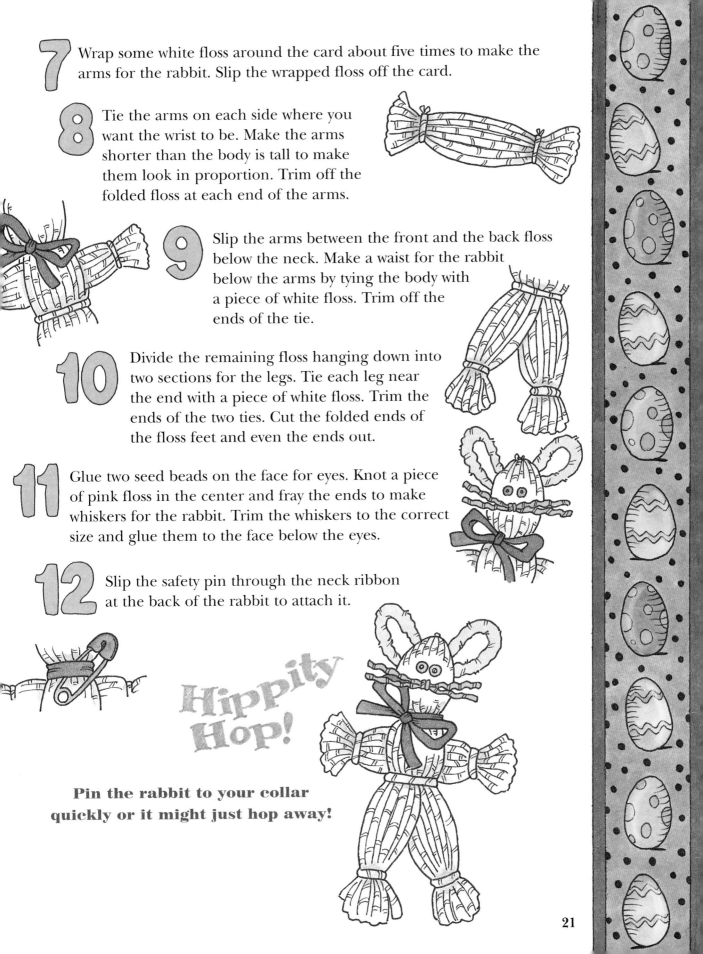

9 Slip the arms between the front and the back floss below the neck. Make a waist for the rabbit below the arms by tying the body with a piece of white floss. Trim off the ends of the tie.

10 Divide the remaining floss hanging down into two sections for the legs. Tie each leg near the end with a piece of white floss. Trim the ends of the two ties. Cut the folded ends of the floss feet and even the ends out.

11 Glue two seed beads on the face for eyes. Knot a piece of pink floss in the center and fray the ends to make whiskers for the rabbit. Trim the whiskers to the correct size and glue them to the face below the eyes.

12 Slip the safety pin through the neck ribbon at the back of the rabbit to attach it.

Hippity Hop!

Pin the rabbit to your collar quickly or it might just hop away!

Make this bunny puppet with a wiggly nose.

Twitching Nose Bunny

Here is what you need:

white craft glue

glue

pencil

scissors

pink yarn

masking tape

ruler

white poster board

two wiggle eyes

small pink pom-pom

old white sock

cotton ball

fiberfill

clear disposable plastic cup

Here is what you do:

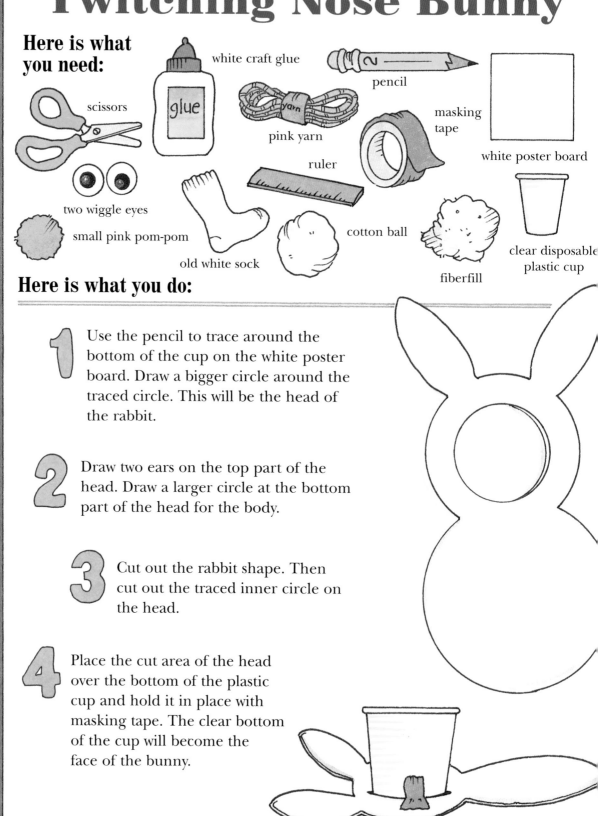

1 Use the pencil to trace around the bottom of the cup on the white poster board. Draw a bigger circle around the traced circle. This will be the head of the rabbit.

2 Draw two ears on the top part of the head. Draw a larger circle at the bottom part of the head for the body.

3 Cut out the rabbit shape. Then cut out the traced inner circle on the head.

4 Place the cut area of the head over the bottom of the plastic cup and hold it in place with masking tape. The clear bottom of the cup will become the face of the bunny.

5 Cover the poster board with glue, then fiberfill, to give the bunny fur. Add a cotton ball tail on one side of the bottom of the body.

6 Place a handful of fiberfill inside the cup. Twist and turn it so that it takes on the shape of the bottom of the cup. Remove the fiberfill from the cup without disturbing the shape.

7 Glue the two wiggle eyes on the flattened fiberfill that shows through the bottom of the cup.

8 Cut a 3-inch (8-cm) piece of yarn. Knot the yarn in the center, then fray the ends to make whiskers for the bunny.

9 Glue the whiskers below the eyes, then glue the pink pom-pom over the center for a nose. When the glue has dried, place the fiberfill back in the cup so that the face shows through the bottom of the cup at the front of the bunny.

10 Cut the cuff off the old sock. Slip the cuff over the cup to help hold the fiberfill in.

To use the puppet, place your hand through the cuff into the cup. Wiggle your fingers around in the fiberfill to make it look like the nose of the bunny is twitching.

23

Make your mom a pretty flower corsage for Easter.

Twist-Tie Flower Corsage

Here is what you need:

thin craft ribbon

green pipe cleaners

scissors

small pom-poms

twist ties in at least two different colors

safety pin

ruler

masking tape

colored map pins

Here is what you do:

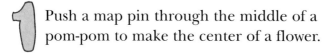

1 Push a map pin through the middle of a pom-pom to make the center of a flower.

2 Push the pin through the center of eight or more twist ties to make the petals of the flower.

3 Tape the part of the pin behind the flower to a 6-inch (15-cm) piece of green pipe cleaner to give the flower a stem. Wrap the tape around and around the pin to cover it and block the sharp point. It is a good idea to do a few extra wraps of masking tape around the point end of the pin to be sure it is well covered.

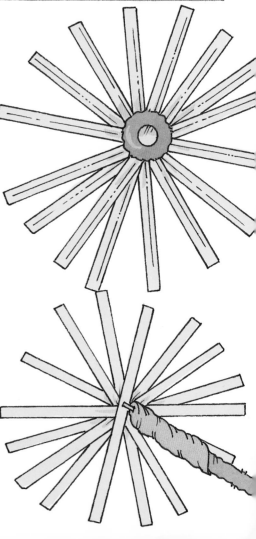

 You can make a smaller flower by omitting the pom-pom center and folding the twist-tie petals in half.

 Make at least three flowers for the corsage.

 Group the flowers together in a pretty arrangement, bending the flower heads forward. Hold them together with a pretty ribbon tied in a bow.

 Trim the flower stems to equal lengths.

 Slip the safety pin through the ribbon at the back of the corsage so that the corsage can be pinned on.

I think your grandma might want one of these charming corsages, too.

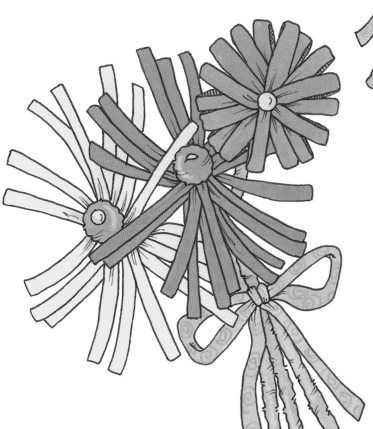

**Plant a few Easter Eggs among your spring plants
or out in the garden.**

"Eggs"-cellent Egg Pokes

Here is what you need:

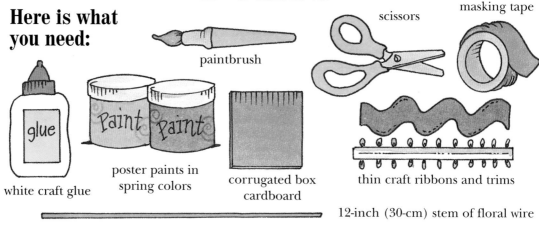

paintbrush

scissors

masking tape

glue

white craft glue

Paint Paint

poster paints in
spring colors

corrugated box
cardboard

thin craft ribbons and trims

12-inch (30-cm) stem of floral wire

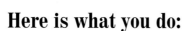

pencil

Plastic Wrap

clear plastic wrap

construction paper

ruler

Here is what you do:

1 Use the pencil to sketch an egg shape from 4 to 6 inches (10 to 15 cm) tall on the corrugated box cardboard. It is important that you sketch the egg with the lines of the cardboard running from the top to the bottom of the egg.

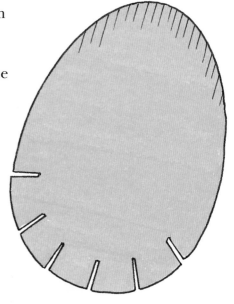

2 Cut the egg shape out and use the poster paint to paint the egg the color of your choice.

3 Cut ½-inch (1.27-cm) slits all the way around the outside of the egg at ½-inch (1.27-cm) intervals.

4 Cut 1- to 3-foot (30- to 91-cm) lengths of the various trims and ribbons.

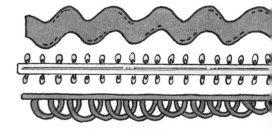

26

5 Attach the end of a trim or ribbon piece in a cut slot, with the end sticking out at the back of the egg. Use masking tape to secure the end if it seems loose.

6 Randomly wrap the egg with the ribbon or trim until it is all used. Make sure that the end is at the back of the egg.

7 Continue wrapping the egg with various trims and ribbons until all the slots have been used at least once and you have a design that you are happy with on the front of the egg.

8 Use masking tape to stick down any loose ends of ribbon or trim at the back of the egg. Trace around the egg on construction paper. Cut the egg shape out. Glue the construction paper egg shape to the back of the egg to cover it.

9 Dip one end of the floral wire in glue. Slide the gluey end up in one of the holes in the cardboard at the bottom of the egg.

10 If you are going to use the egg outside you will need to cover it with a square of plastic wrap. Tie the wrap at the bottom of the egg with a piece of ribbon tied in a bow.

Make lots of these pretty eggs to "plant" for the Easter season.

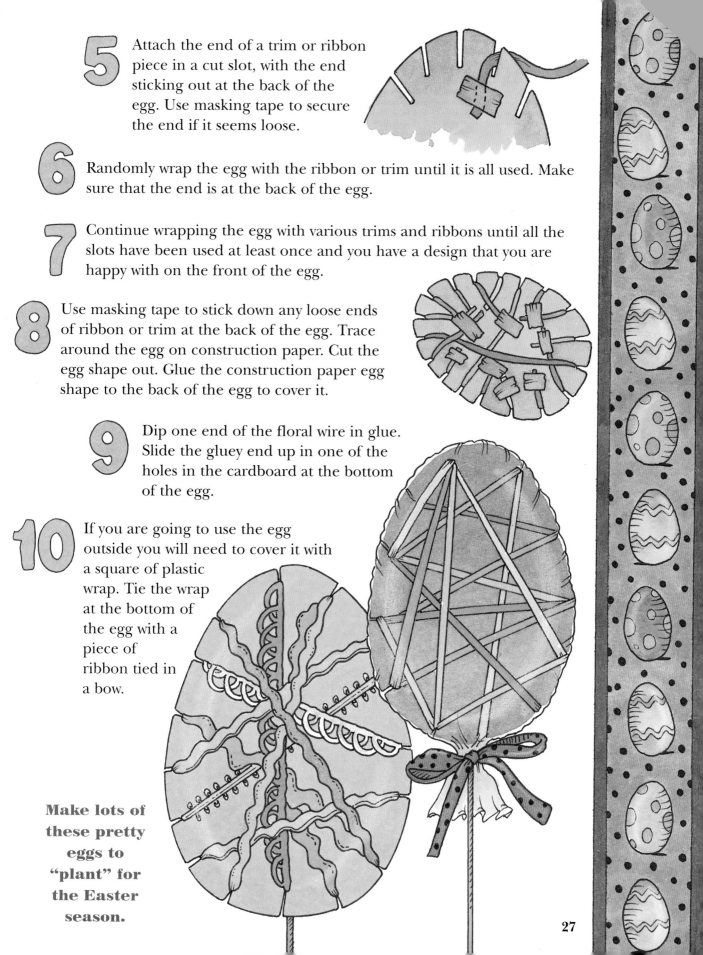

Decorate your door with a pretty spring wreath.

Basket of Flowers Door Wreath

Here is what you need:

white craft glue

small hole punch

two uncoated 9-inch (23-cm) paper plates

large paper clip

yellow poster paint

newspaper to work on

paper fasteners

paintbrush

scissors

masking tape

ruler

½ to 1-inch (1.25 to 2.5-cm) -wide ribbons in green and other colors

Here is what you do:

1 To make the basket handle, cut the center out of one paper plate.

2 Cut the second paper plate in half.

3 Glue one of the halves, flat side up, to the bottom third of the circle handle to form the basket. Paint the entire plate basket yellow.

4 To make a flower, cut three 4-inch (10-cm) pieces of green ribbon and four 4-inch pieces of another color ribbon.

4 inches

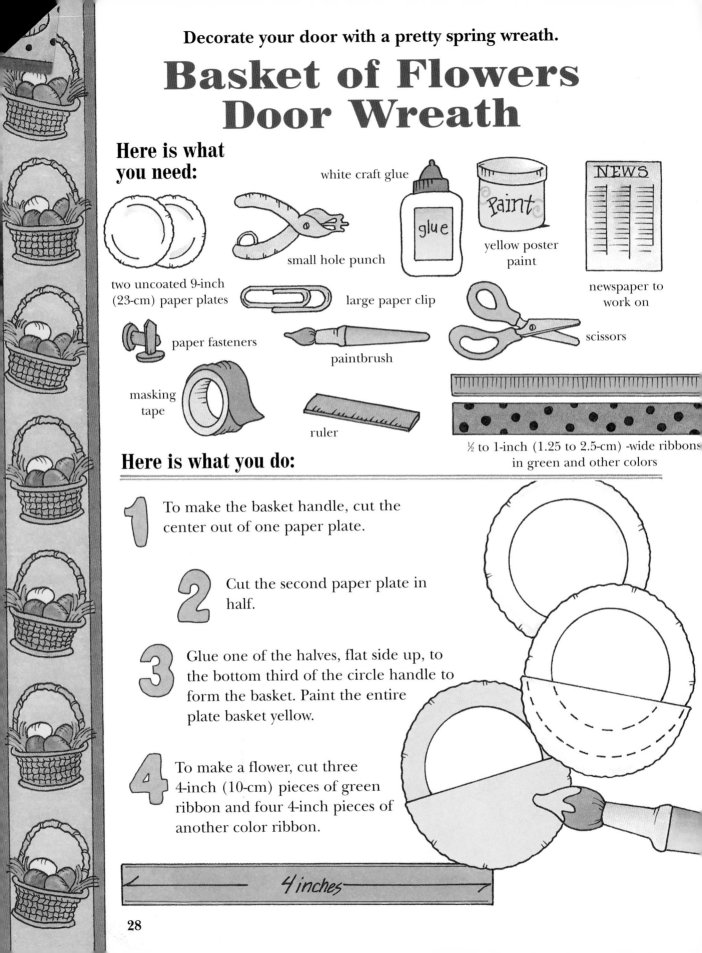

5 Punch a hole in the center of each piece of colored ribbon. Thread the ribbon on the end of a paper fastener so that the top of the fastener becomes the center of the flower. If the flower ribbon is more than ½ inch (1.27 cm) wide, you might want to fold it in half and punch a hole through both layers. Threading it on the fastener will then hold the fold in place at the center.

6 Punch a hole in the center of each green piece of ribbon and thread them on the paper fastener to form the back part of the flower. Make three different flowers.

7 Punch three holes along the top of the plate basket.

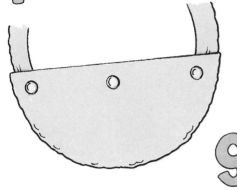

8 Attach each of the three flowers to the basket by putting each paper fastener through a hole and bending the ends out in back of the basket to secure it.

9 Tie a piece of ribbon in a bow. Glue the bow to the top side of the handle of the basket.

10 Glue the large paper clip to the back of the handle, sticking up from the top, to form a hanger for the basket. Secure the glued paper clip with a piece of masking tape.

These easy to make and decorative flowers are perfect for decorating the Easter basket that is found on page 6.

Make a flock of spring lambs.

Spring Lamb Finger Puppet

Here is what you need:

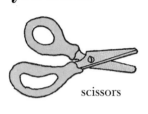
scissors

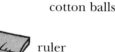
white craft glue

black pipe cleaner

cotton balls

thin craft ribbon

blue and pink seed beads

ruler

marker cap from fat black marker

Here is what you do:

1 Spread out two or three cotton balls.

2 Cover the outside of the marker cap with glue. Wrap the cap in the cotton to make the body of the sheep.

3 Glue the two blue seed beads to the end of the cap for eyes.

4 Glue the pink seed bead below the eyes for a nose.

5 Cut three 2-inch (5-cm) pieces of the black pipe cleaner. Fold one piece of pipe cleaner in half. Fold the two ends in half again to shape ears for the sheep.

6 Glue the ears to the edge of the cap above the eyes.

7 Bend the other two pieces of pipe cleaner in half to form legs for the sheep.

8 Glue the fold of each pair of legs to the bottom of the sheep. Trim the legs so that the sheep will stand.

9 Tie a piece of ribbon in a bow around the neck of the sheep.

Baa, Baa...

This lamb is the perfect size to use when playing with the bunny family on page 14.

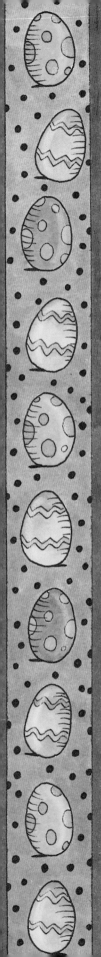

Bet you can't make just one of these!

Eggshell Flowers

Here is what you need:

white craft glue

egg dye, food coloring, or poster paint

paintbrush

scissors

glue

small pom-poms

green and yellow pipe cleaners

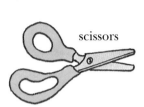 washed eggshell halves saved from cooking

ballpoint pen

Here is what you do:

1 To make a flower, use the pen to carefully poke a small hole in the center of the bottom of the eggshell.

2 Color the eggshell by dipping it in egg dye or water dyed with a few drops of food coloring. You can also paint the eggshell with poster paint.

3 Cut a pipe cleaner stem about 6 inches (15 cm) long.

6 inches

4 Poke the end of the pipe cleaner through the hole in the eggshell. Fold the end of the pipe cleaner to one side in the cup of the egg and secure it with glue.

5 Glue a pom-pom over the folded pipe cleaner end to conceal it and form a center for the flower.

6 To make a different center for the flower, cut a 3-inch (8-cm) piece of yellow pipe cleaner.

7 Bend the yellow piece of pipe cleaner in half, then tip the two ends out to look like a flower stamen.

8 Poke the green pipe cleaner through the hole in the egg. Fold the end of the pipe cleaner around the folded center of the yellow stamen. Pull the base of the stamen down to the bottom of the inside of the egg cup and secure it with glue.

Make a bouquet of different eggshell flowers. Display the flowers in a pretty container (try covering a paper cup with a patterned sock) with some fake greenery tucked in to enhance the arrangement.

pretty!

These little hatching chicks are sure to bring a smile to anyone who sees them.

Hatching Chick Wobblers

Here is what you need:

two wiggle eyes

white craft glue

ruler

scissors

pencil

large yellow pom-pom

two washed eggshells that have been emptied from the small end

two jingle bells

egg dye (optional)

Play-Doh modeling compound

orange pipe cleaner

yellow craft feather fluffs

Here is what you do:

1 Ask a grown-up to save you some eggshells that have been opened and emptied from the small end. It is easy to crack the eggs this way when using them for cooking.

2 Roll a marble-size ball of Play-Doh. Drop the Play-Doh ball into the egg and use the eraser end of the pencil to gently press the Play-Doh onto the bottom of the egg, slightly off center. This will cause the egg to stand and bob around.

3 Drop a jingle bell into each egg to create a pecking sound when the egg is shaken.

4 To make the chick hatching headfirst, stuff the yellow pom-pom into one egg to look like the head of a chick.

5 Glue the two wiggle eyes to the pom-pom. Cut a 1-inch (2.5-cm)-long piece of orange pipe cleaner. Bend the pipe cleaner in half to form a beak for the chick.

6 Glue the beak to the pom-pom below the eyes.

7 To make the chick hatching feetfirst, stuff some feather fluffs into the egg, stems first.

8 Cut a 4-inch (10-cm) piece of orange pipe cleaner. Bend the pipe cleaner in half to form the two legs for the chick.

9 Cut two 1-inch (2.5-cm) pieces of orange pipe cleaner. Wrap a piece around the end part of each leg to form feet for the chick.

10 Dip the folded top of the two legs in glue, then put it inside the eggshell between the feather fluffs so that the two legs stick out of the shell.

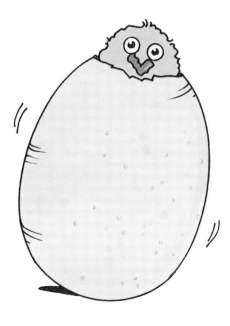

These funny wobblers make a delightful Easter gift. 35

Here is a charming idea for a table favor.

Bird's Nest Favor

Here is what you need:

white craft glue

craft feather fluff (small craft feathers)

glue

pencil

½-inch and 1-inch (1.25- and 2.5-cm) pom-pom of same color

Play-Doh modeling compound

scissors

Easter grass

washed eggshells broken and emptied from the small end

two seed beads

orange felt scrap

small wrapped chocolate eggs

ruler

Here is what you do:

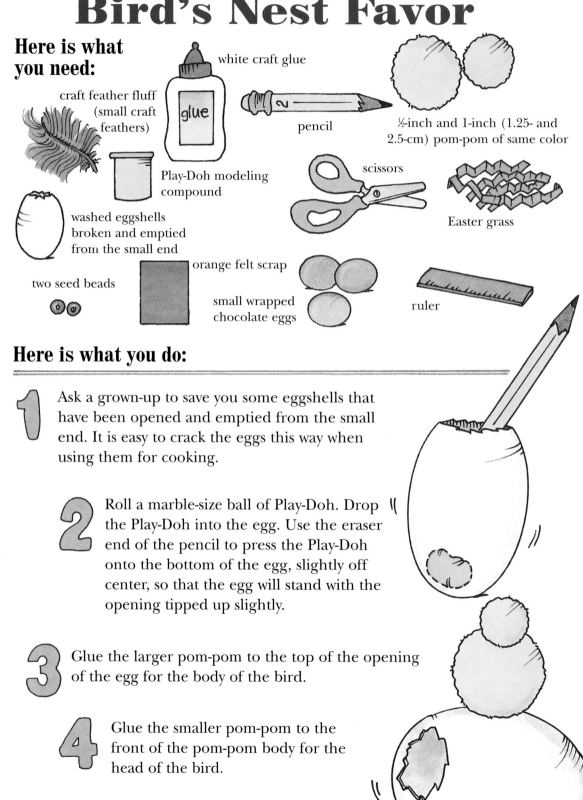

1. Ask a grown-up to save you some eggshells that have been opened and emptied from the small end. It is easy to crack the eggs this way when using them for cooking.

2. Roll a marble-size ball of Play-Doh. Drop the Play-Doh into the egg. Use the eraser end of the pencil to press the Play-Doh onto the bottom of the egg, slightly off center, so that the egg will stand with the opening tipped up slightly.

3. Glue the larger pom-pom to the top of the opening of the egg for the body of the bird.

4. Glue the smaller pom-pom to the front of the pom-pom body for the head of the bird.

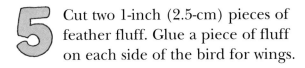
5 Cut two 1-inch (2.5-cm) pieces of feather fluff. Glue a piece of fluff on each side of the bird for wings.

6 Glue the two seed beads to the head of the bird for eyes. Cut a small triangle-shaped beak from the felt scrap. Glue the beak to the head of the bird below the eyes.

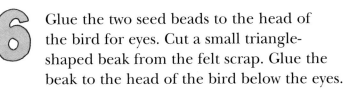

7 You may need to use the pencil to rearrange the Play-Doh so that the bird is balanced at the top of the opening of the egg.

8 Tuck some Easter grass inside the egg, then add some wrapped chocolate eggs.

If you do not want the egg nest to bob around, you can omit the Play-Doh and stand it on a small plastic cap from a soda or salad-dressing bottle. You might want to glue some trim around the cap to decorate it.

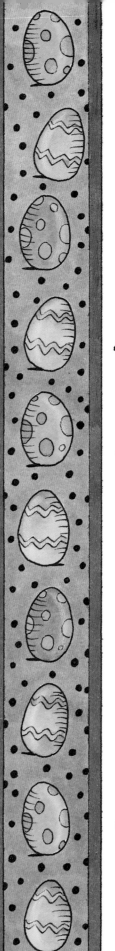

This garland is perfect for decorating an egg tree or houseplant.

Ribbon Flowers Garland

Here is what you need:

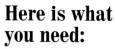
tiny pom-poms

glue
white craft glue

ruler

two pony beads

scissors

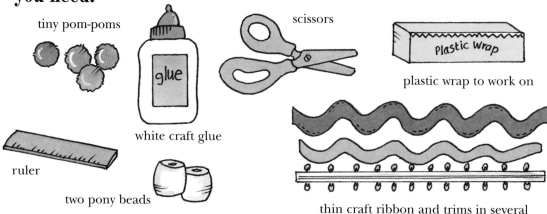
Plastic Wrap
plastic wrap to work on

thin craft ribbon and trims in several spring colors

Here is what you do:

1 Cut a 3-foot (90-cm) length of ribbon to use as the base for the garland.

2 Fold one end of the ribbon over and knot it to make a hook at one end of the garland for hanging it on a branch or plant.

3 Slip a pony bead over the folded end, then knot it again to hold the bead in place.

4 Tear off a strip of plastic wrap as long as the base ribbon. Lay the ribbon flat across the plastic wrap so you will have a nonstick surface to work on.

5 To make each flower, cut four 1½- to 2-inch (4- to 5-cm) pieces of ribbon or trim.

6 Glue the ribbon or trim pieces to the base ribbon with the strips crossing over each other to form a flower.

7 Glue a pom-pom in the center of the flower.

8 Make a flower every 4 to 5 inches (10 to 13 cm) along the ribbon.

9 When you reach the end of the ribbon, fold and knot the end to make a hanger for that end, too. Add the second pony bead and knot the ribbon again to hold it in place.

You can make a longer garland or several shorter ones using different color ribbons for the base.

This egg has a duck hatching out of it, but you might want to make something different hatch out of the egg.

Hatching Duck Puppet

Here is what you need:

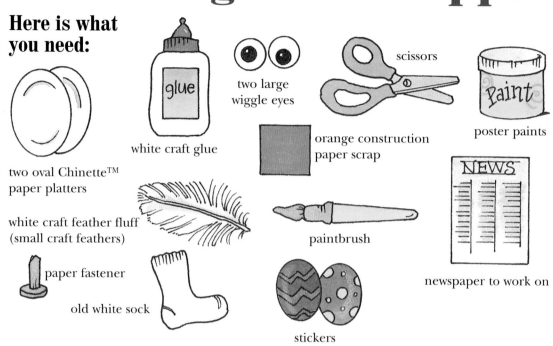

two oval Chinette™ paper platters

white craft glue

two large wiggle eyes

scissors

poster paints

orange construction paper scrap

white craft feather fluff (small craft feathers)

paintbrush

NEWS

newspaper to work on

paper fastener

old white sock

stickers

Here is what you do:

1 Cut across the top third of one of the platters in a zigzag pattern to look like a broken egg.

2 Turn the uncut platter, food side up, so that it looks like an egg.

3 Glue the large half of the cut platter, food side down, over the bottom of the other platter.

4 Attach the top part of the cut platter to the left side of the bottom platter using a paper fastener. The platters should now look like an egg with the top opening and closing on the fastener.

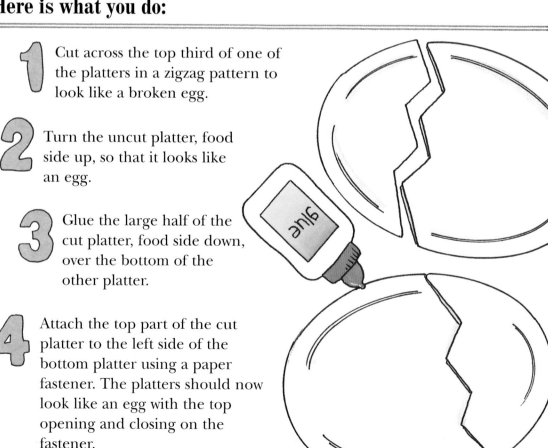

40

5 You can paint the inside portion of the top of the egg or leave it white. Paint the outside of the egg. When the egg is dry, decorate it with stickers.

6 Cut a hole large enough to fit your hand through in the lower half of the back of the egg.

7 Stick the foot of the sock through the hole in the back of the egg so that the top of the foot becomes the front of the puppet.

8 Glue the base of the puppet to the back of the egg to secure it. Trim away the excess sock.

9 Glue the two wiggle eyes to the front of the puppet. Glue the feather fluff to the head of the puppet above the eyes. Fold the orange paper in half. Cut a duck bill on the fold so that it has a top and a bottom bill. Glue the bottom bill to the puppet just below the eyes.

To use the puppet, put your hand inside the sock duck and close the top of the egg. Work your hand inside the sock to make the duck open the top part of the egg to "hatch."

Quack!

This little angel is made entirely from egg shapes.

Egg Angel Wall Hanging

Here is what you need:

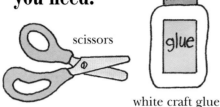
scissors

glue

white craft glue

markers

gold sparkle stem

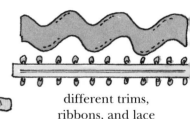
different trims, ribbons, and lace

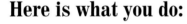
clamp clothespin

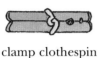
yarn

yarn bits for hair

construction paper in several pastel colors

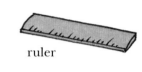
ruler

sequins and seed beads

Here is what you do:

1 Cut two identical 6-inch (15-cm)-tall egg shapes for wings and a third egg the same size, but in a different color, for the dress.

2 Glue the two wings on the top portion of a sheet of paper with the small ends touching.

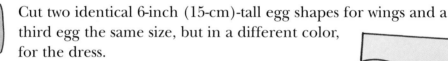

3 Decorate the egg-shapes with strips of lace, ribbon, and trim to make them look like Easter eggs. Decorate the third egg in the same way.

4 Glue the small end of the third egg over the center part of the wings, small end up, for the dress.

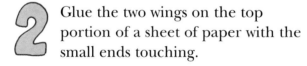

5 Cut two smaller egg shapes for the sleeves of the dress. Slip the end of each sleeve under a side of the dress. Cut two small egg shapes for hands. Glue the hands to the front of the ends of the sleeves.

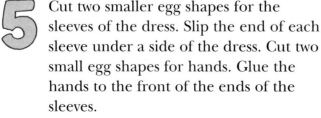

42

6 Cut a smaller egg shape for the head. Glue the head to the top part of the dress. Use the markers to give the angel a face. Glue yarn bits to the top of the head for hair. Shape the sparkle stem into a circle to make a halo. Trim off any excess. Glue the back of the halo behind the top of the angel's head so that it sticks out in front.

7 Cut an egg from construction paper for the angel to hold. Use the trims, sequins, and seed beads to decorate the egg. Pull the hands of the angel forward and glue them to each side of the egg to look like the angel is holding the egg. Secure the hands with clamp clothespins until the glue has dried.

8 Cut a 24-inch (61-cm) length of ribbon. Knot the two ends of the ribbon together to make a hanger for the angel.

9 Fold back about 1 inch (2.5 cm) of paper at the top of the angel. Slide one side of the hanger under the fold and secure the fold with glue. Use clamp clothespins to hold it until the glue is dry.

10 Decorate the paper edges that the angel is glued on with strips of trim, lace, and ribbon.

Have fun creatively decorating the egg shapes you use to make the angel.

Serve snacks to your holiday guests in an Easter bonnet!

Easter Bonnet Snack Dish

Here is what you need:

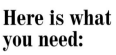
scissors

artificial flowers

two identical disposable plastic bowls

organdy ribbon

thin plastic from a shopping bag or disposable plastic tablecloth

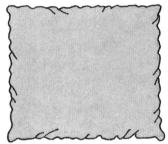

Here is what you do:

1 Cut a square of plastic that is large enough to cover the outside of the bowl and stick out about 3 inches (8 cm) around the bowl.

2 Cover the bottom of one bowl with the plastic square. Secure it by slipping the second bowl over the first with the plastic in between.

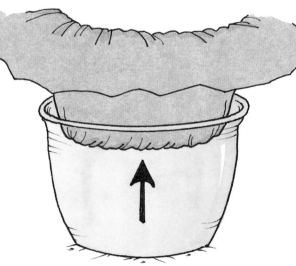

44

3 Arrange the plastic evenly around the inner bowl, then fold the edges out.

4 Trim the edges into a circle around the bowl to look like the brim of a hat.

5 Tie a piece of organdy ribbon around the bowl.

6 Tie some artificial flowers to the ribbon, then tie the ribbon in a bow.

Make several different "bonnets" to fill with Easter candy and snacks.

Yum-Yum!

Make place cards for all your Easter guests.

Bunny and Basket Place Card

Here is what you need:

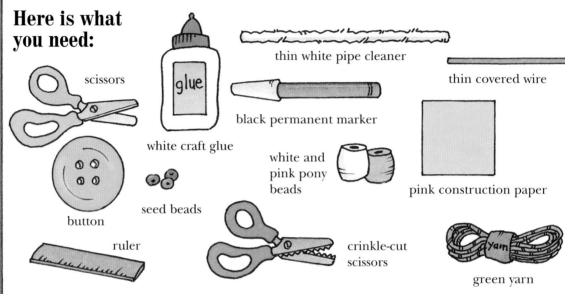

scissors

white craft glue

glue

thin white pipe cleaner

thin covered wire

black permanent marker

button

seed beads

white and pink pony beads

pink construction paper

ruler

crinkle-cut scissors

green yarn

yarn

Here is what you do:

1 Make a tiny bunny by folding a 2-inch (5-cm) piece of white pipe cleaner in half and threading two white pony beads on the folded end.

2 Fold the two ends of the pipe cleaner out to form ears. Trim the ends as needed. Use the black marker to draw a face on the bunny.

3 Cut bits of the green yarn to use for grass. Glue the yarn bits to one side of the button. Glue the bunny to the yarn grass on the button.

4 Fold a 1-inch (2.5-cm) piece of covered wire in half. Dip the ends of the wire in glue, then slip them in one end of the pink pony bead to look like the handle of a basket.

5 Glue the basket in the yarn grass next to the bunny. Glue some tiny seed beads to the top of the basket to look like colored Easter eggs.

6 Use the scissors to cut a 2- by 3-inch (5- by 8-cm) rectangle from the pink construction paper. Use the crinkle-cut scissors to trim around the paper if you want to give the rectangle a fancy edge.

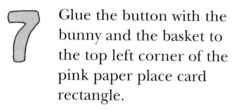

7 Glue the button with the bunny and the basket to the top left corner of the pink paper place card rectangle.

8 Use the marker to write the name of the person you are going to use the place card for on the paper.

Make a pretty place card for each person at your Easter table. Try using different color beads for each of the baskets.

Jim

About the Author and Artist

Thirty years as a teacher and director of nursery school programs have given Kathy Ross extensive experience in guiding young children through craft projects. Among the more than forty craft books she has written are *Crafts for All Seasons, Make Yourself a Monster, Crafts From Your Favorite Children's Songs, Kathy Ross Crafts Letter Shapes,* and *Star-Spangled Crafts.* To find out more about Kathy, visit her Web site: *www.kathyross.com.*

Sharon Lane Holm, a resident of New Fairfield, Connecticut, won awards for her work in advertising design before shifting her concentration to children's books. Her recent books include *Sidewalk Games Around the World; Happy Birthday, Everywhere!; Happy New Year, Everywhere!;* and *Merry Christmas, Everywhere!,* all by Arlene Erlbach; and *Beautiful Bats* by Linda Glaser.

Together, Kathy Ross and Sharon Lane Holm have also created *The Best Christmas Crafts Ever!,* as well as the popular Holiday Crafts for Kids series and the Crafts for Kids Who Are Wild About series.